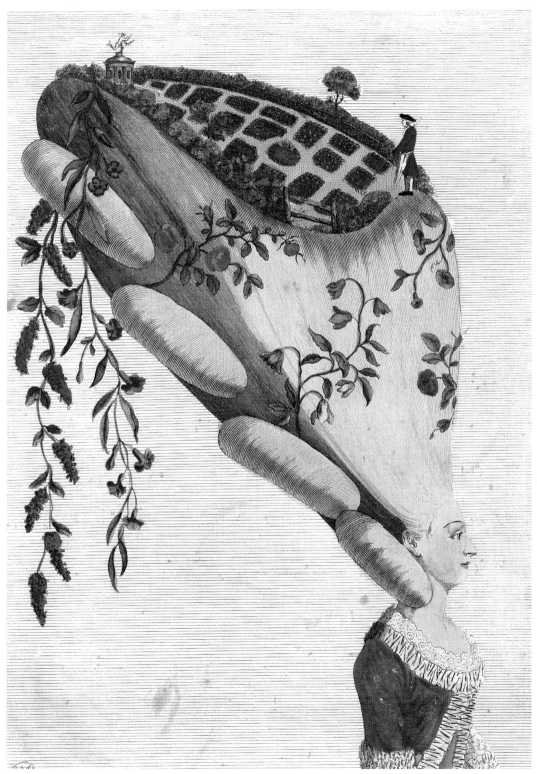

The Flower Garden (detail). Published by Matthias Darly, British, active ca. 1740–1770s.

If you think these cows are enjoying a pleasant day on the farm—

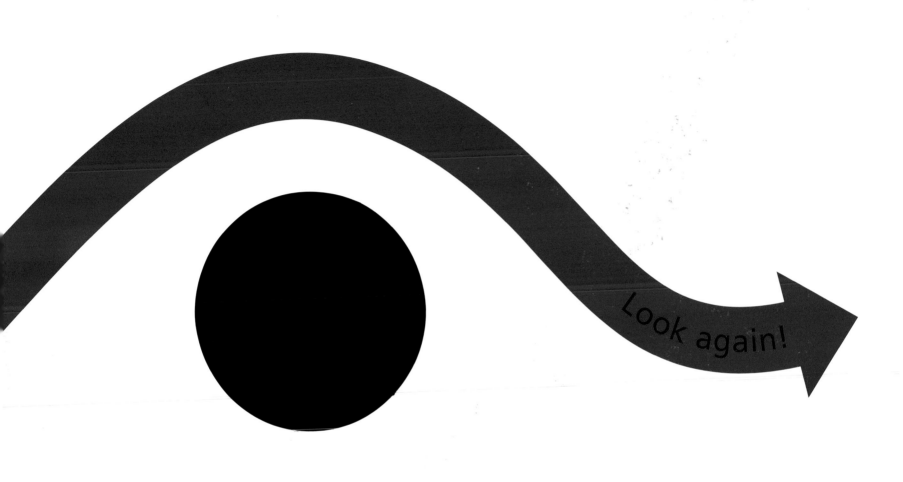

Look again!

The cows are in an art gallery! While several observers wait to see how the "real" cow will respond to the "painted" cows, a man with a mop waits to see if . . . well, you know. But why would anyone care how a cow reacts to a painting of a cow? Could the artist be poking fun at art critics?

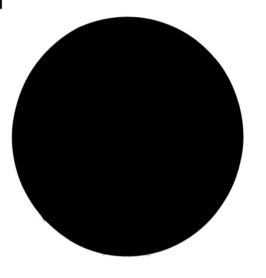

The Innocent Eye Test. Mark Tansey, American, b. 1949.

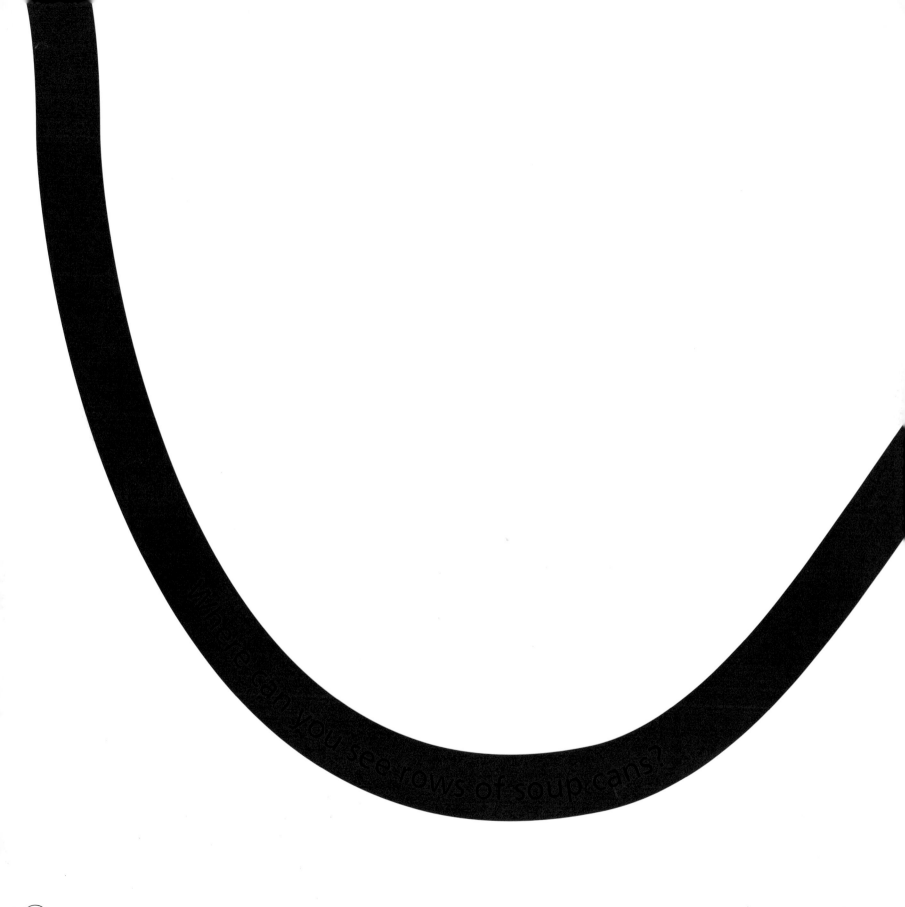

Where can you see rows of soup cans?

In a grocery store? A pantry? Look again!

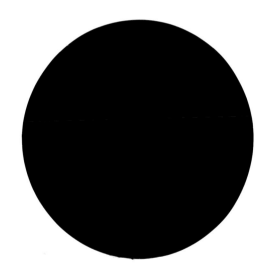

The soup cans are printed on a dress! In 1962, Andy Warhol painted thirty-two pictures of a Campbell's soup can, one for each flavor the company made. Four years later, Campbell Soup Company promoted its products with "*The Souper Dress*," a throw-away paper dress featuring the cans that inspired Warhol's work. The dress cost one dollar plus two soup-can labels. Today, a 1960s "Souper Dress" in good shape can cost several thousand dollars!

"The Souper Dress." American, ca. 1966–67.

Have you see a young woman delicately holding a flower

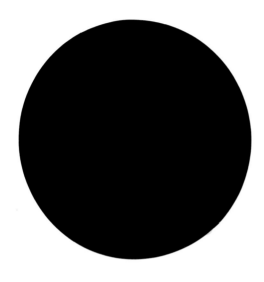

Or do you?

Look again!

The "woman" is really a Hindu god called Krishna. The god is shown as a creature made up of different animals. It has the head and neck of a peacock, the hump of a bull, and the body of a lion. It has a snake for a tail and only three legs: one each from an elephant, a tiger, and a deer. In place of the fourth leg is a woman's arm. This form of the god shows that Krishna is everything at once and can never be known completely.

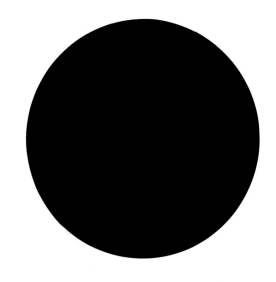

नवकुँजर

Navagunjara, a Universal Form of Krishna. Indian (Rajasthan, Jodhpur[?]), ca. 1835.

Someone is reaching into his pocket to get something.

Or is he?

Look again!

It's a woman picking a young nobleman's pocket while a fortune teller distracts him. And that's not all! Another woman is cutting the chain that holds the man's heavy gold medal while keeping an eye on him to make sure he doesn't catch her. But it doesn't look like she has to worry. The man is so busy keeping *his* eye on the fortune teller, he has no idea what else is going on around him.

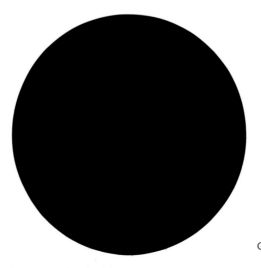

The Fortune Teller (detail).
Georges de La Tour, French,
1593–1652.

Nothing stirs on this rocky beach overlooking a tranquil sea

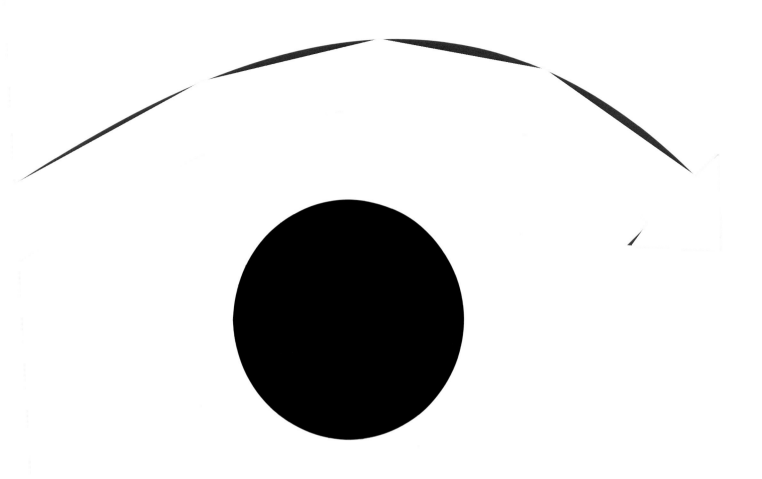

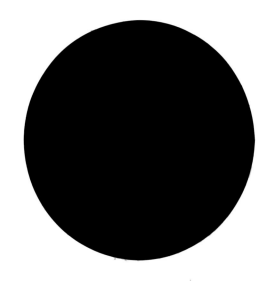

The rocks are actually the back of a huge sea serpent! Hundreds of people reported sighting along the New England coast during the 1800s. Though many took it seriously, others joked about it. Just as witnesses couldn't agree on the size of sea serpent, the painter, Elihu Vedder, has left the length of the creature a mystery.

Lair of the Sea Serpent (detail). Elihu Vedder, American, 1836–1923.

Is this camouflage on a soldier's uniform?

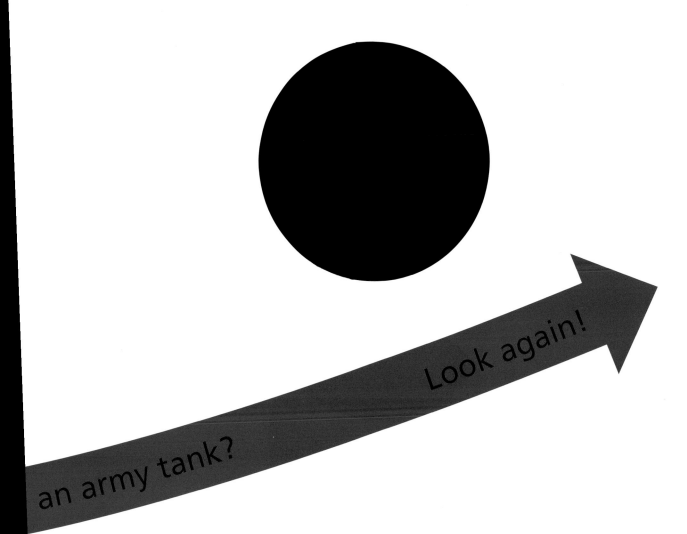

an army tank?

Look again!

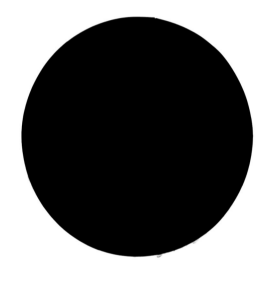

It's on the arti
Does a self-po
reveal the arti
personality or
it? Andy War
a Pop artist w
his own name
face as famili
pictures of ce
and Campbel
cans. In this p
however, he
camouflage
Why do you
might have

Self-Portrait. A

26

On a pleasant summer evening, sailboats drift across the still waters of a bay.

Or do they?

Look again!

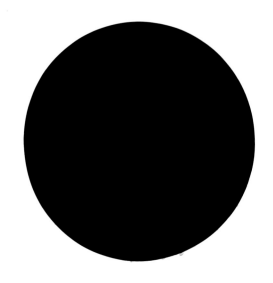

The sailboats *are* out on a pleasant summer evening, but instead of drifting across a bay, they're cupped in a huge goblet. The title of the painting, *The Titan's Goblet*, suggests it was made by a giant. Other than that, the artist left no record of what he was thinking when he painted this. One critic suggested that the goblet stands for the human world set down in the vastness of nature. What do you think it means?

The Titan's Goblet (detail). Thomas Cole, American, 1801–1848.

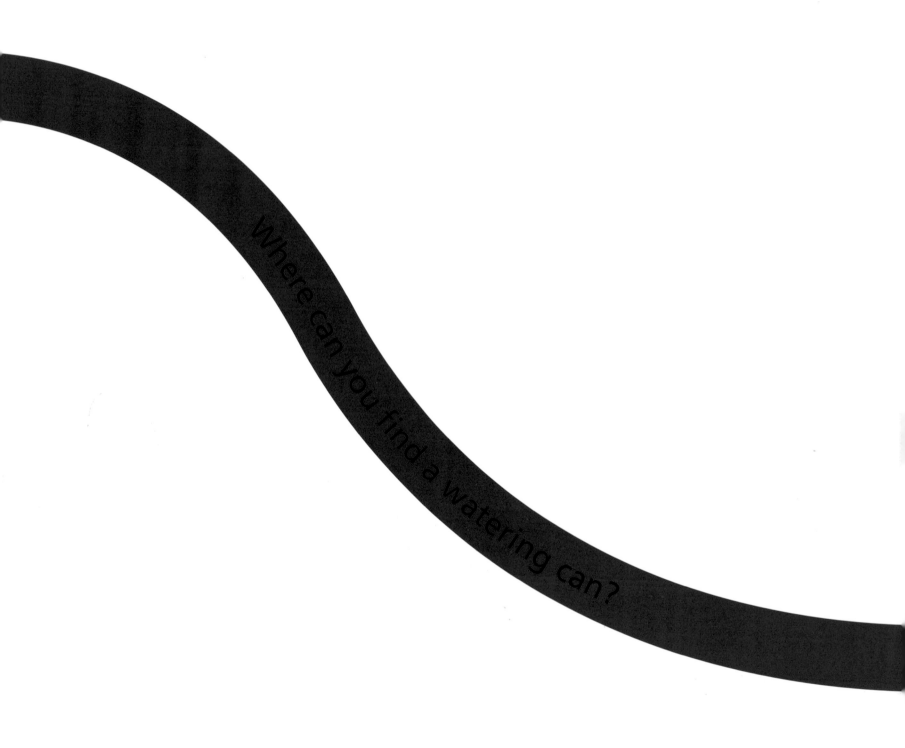

Where can you find a watering can?

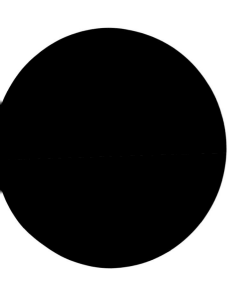

In a garden shed?

A barn?

Look again!

The watering can is in a ballet studio! Were the dancers busy gardening before they rushed to rehearsal? Actually, a watering can was used to sprinkle water on the studio floor to help keep the dust down. The artist included the can as a visual joke—its shape echoes the pose of the dancer on the right.

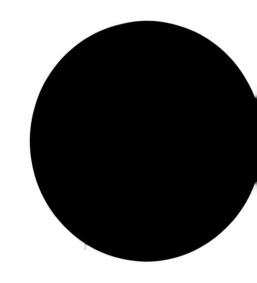

Dancers Practicing at the Barre. Edgar Degas, French, 1834–1917.

What could this be? Perhaps the fringe of a shawl fluttering in the breeze?

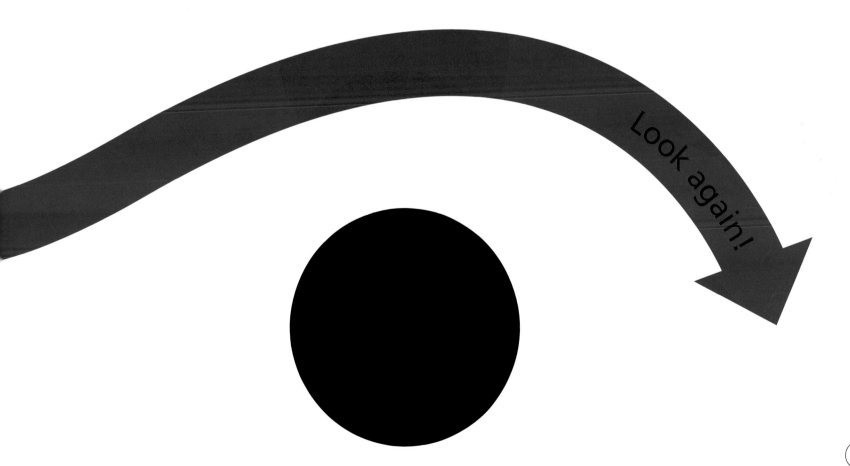

Look again!

It's not fringe but the long fingernails of a *luohan*, or Buddhist holy man, who could perform magic and miracles. The long nails on his fingers and toes (to either side of his upturned hand) show that the holy man is completely detached from worldly concerns, including the need to use his hands or feet.

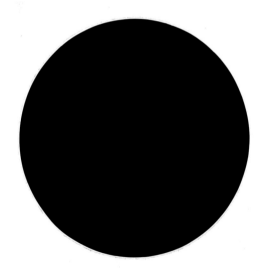

The Sixteen Luohans (detail).
Wu Bin, Chinese, active ca. 1583–1626.

Here is a woman peering out from behind a screen.

Or is she?

Look again!

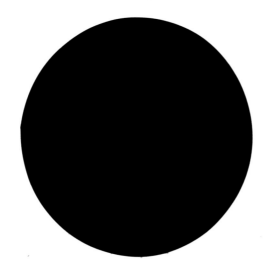

She's not behind a screen but tucked under the rim of an ear painted with overlapping dots. Salvador Dalí designed his painting to look different depending on how far away you stand. If you stand very close, the dots are all you can see. Stand back a few feet and you can see a woman and child. Stand way back and all you can see is the ear. Look at the cherry and the two pieces of paper to the left. Do you think they are part of the painting or attached to it?

Madonna. Salvador Dalí, Spanish, 1904–1989.

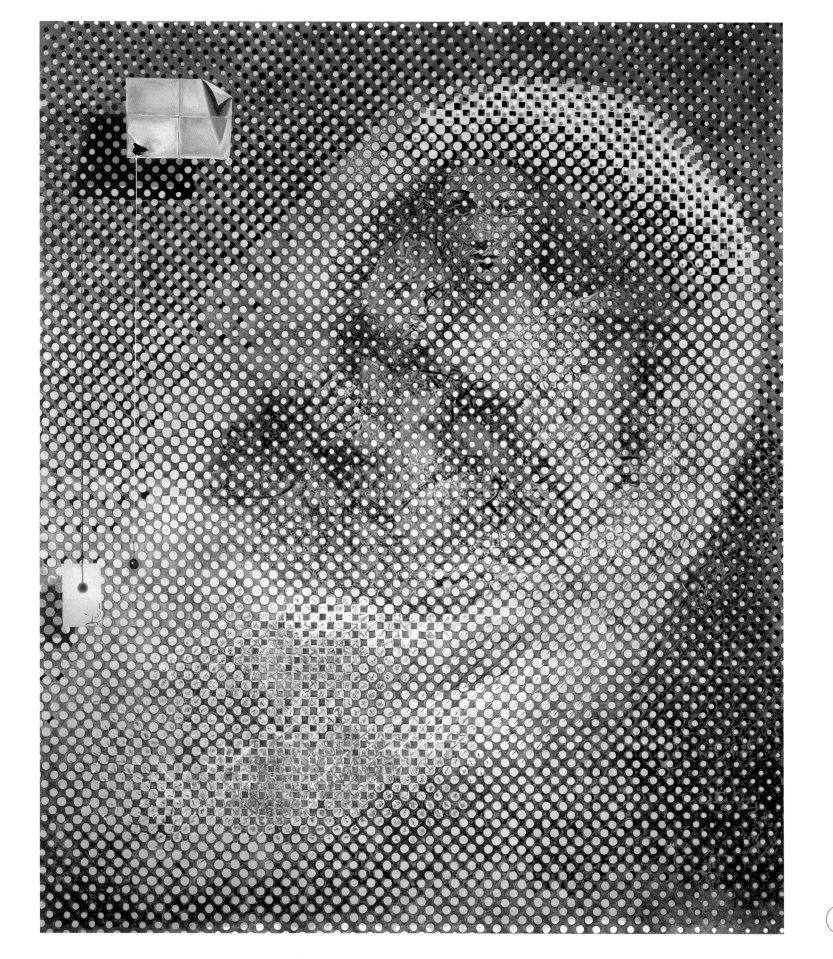

What is this animal fox wearing?

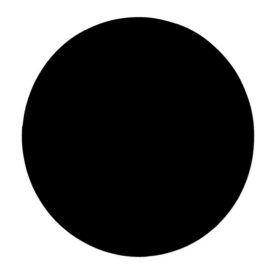

Could it be a turban? Look again!

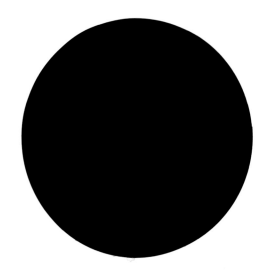

It's a magical fox wearing the disguise of a man. Or is it? The fox's trick takes place in a play, which means that onstage, a male actor must play the part of the fox that's disguised as a man. So did the artist paint a man that's really a fox—or a man that's playing a fox pretending to be a man? Would it make a difference in how you look at the print?

A Fox Dance from the Drama The Thousand Cherry Trees (detail).
Ippitsusai Bunchō, Japanese, 1723–1792.

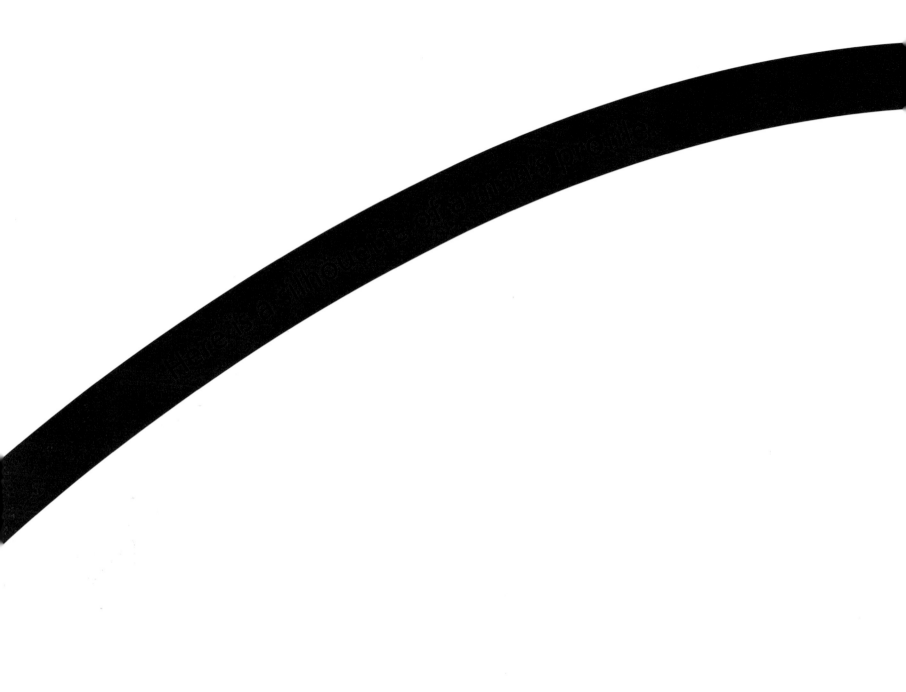

Here's a silhouette of an animal's profile.

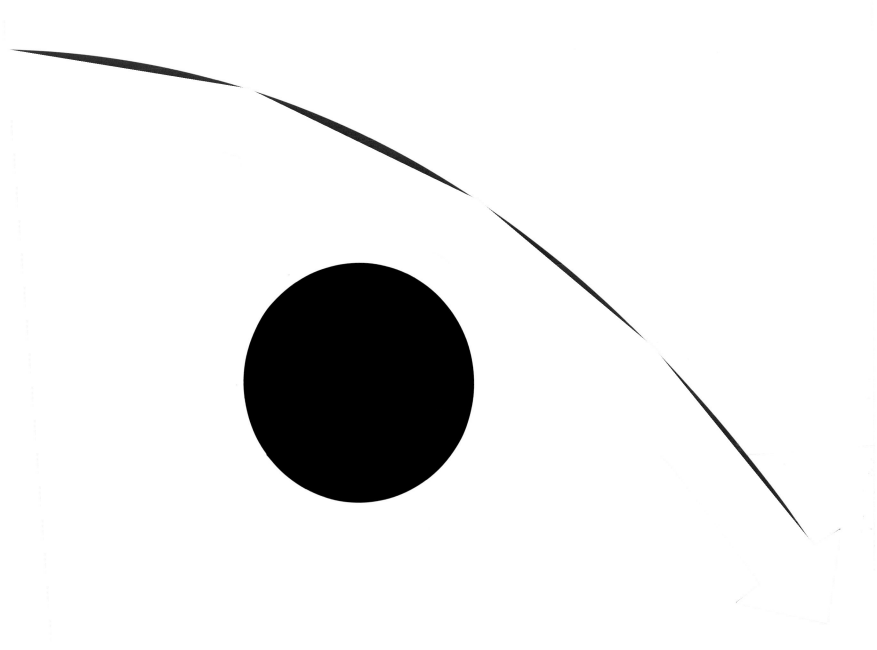

It is a man's profile, but it's also an optical illusion. The profile was formed by the way the artist shaped the tree trunk. Can you find any other profiles in the art? Can you focus on the tree and the profiles at the same time or do you have to look at them separately?

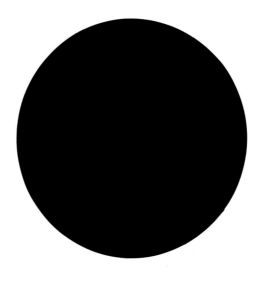

The Royal Allied Oak and Self-Created Mushroom Kings (detail). A
to William Heath, British, 1795–1840, after J. Field, British, early 19t

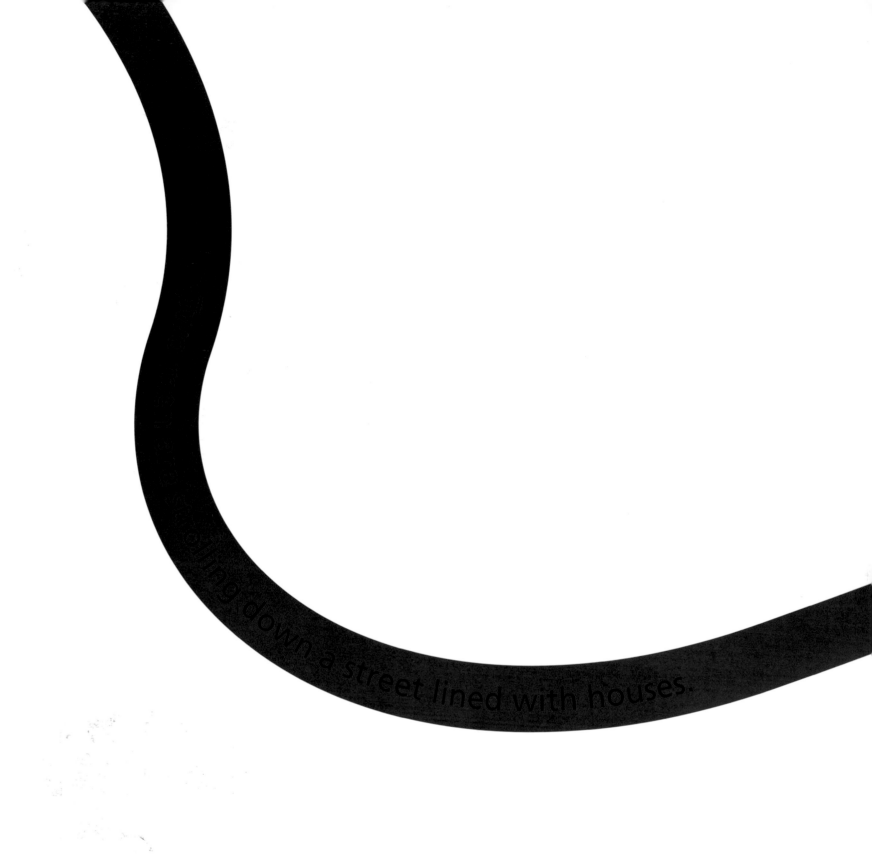

strolling down a street lined with houses.

But is that the whole story?

Look again!

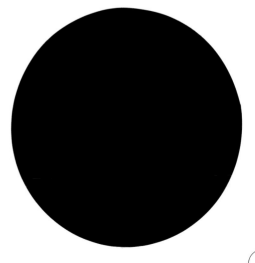

The men, who are actually "outside" the painting, are reflections in a mirror on the counter of a goldsmith's shop. The artist, Petrus Christus, used this trick to pull viewers into his painting. He wanted them to feel as if they were standing at the shop's counter, with the men in the street behind them reflected in the mirror.

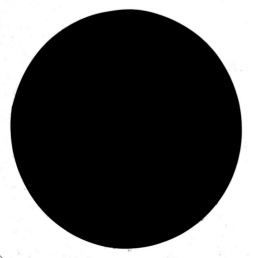

A Goldsmith in His Shop, Possibly Saint Eligius (detail).
Petrus Christus, Netherlandish, active by 1444, died 1475/76.

If you think this is a simple painting of two animals and a man holding a pole...

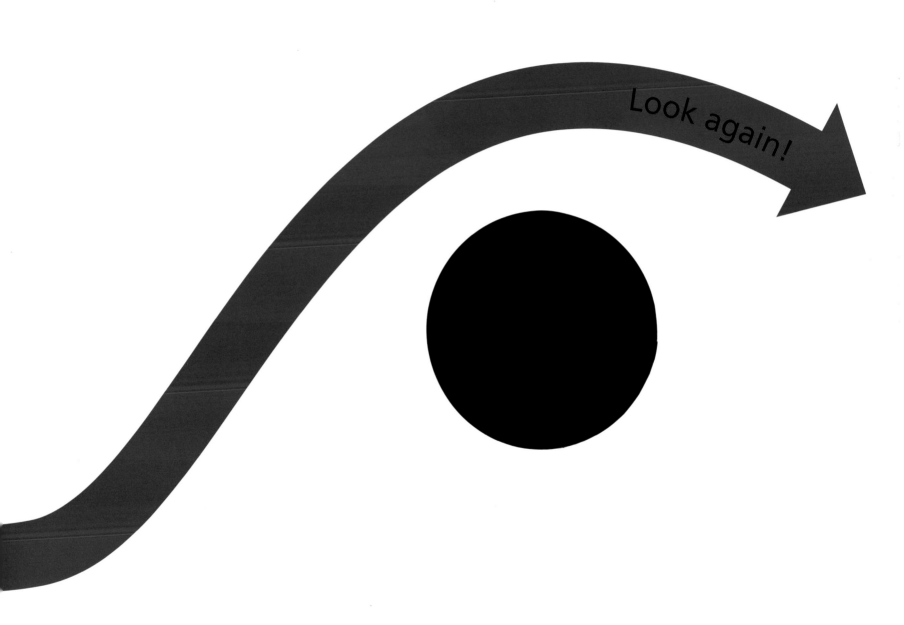

Look again!

In this small painting, the artist fit people and animals together like the pieces of a jigsaw puzzle to make a camel. This picture was painted in the 1500s, but composing an animal's body from other animals and humans was popular in Southwest Asia and India into the 1800s.

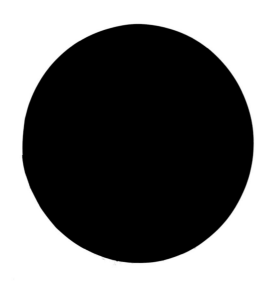

Composite Camel with Attendant (detail). Attributed to Uzbekistan (Bukhara), Safavid Period (1501–1722), 16th century.

The works of art in this book are from the collection of The Metropolitan Museum of Art.

The Flower Garden
Published by Matthias Darly, British,
active ca.1740–1770s
Hand-colored etching, 17¾ x 10¾ in., 1777
Harris Brisbane Dick Fund, 1941   41.25.4

The Innocent Eye Test
Mark Tansey, American, b. 1949
Oil on canvas, 6 ft. 6 in. x 10 ft., 1981
Partial and Promised Gift of Jan Cowles
and Charles Cowles, in honor of William
S. Lieberman, 1988   1988.183
Photograph by D. James Dee
© Mark Tansey

"The Souper Dress"
American, ca. 1966–67
Paper printed with allover pattern
of Campbell's soup cans in black, red,
and gold, L. 32 in.
Purchase, Isabel Schults Fund and Martin and
Caryl Horwitz and Hearst Corporation Gifts,
1995   1995.178.3
The *Campbell's* trademark and red and white
can are used with permission of Campbell
Soup Company.

Navagunjara, a Universal Form of Krishna
Indian (Rajasthan, Jodhpur[?]), ca. 1835
Opaque watercolor, ink, and gold on paper, 8 x 10¼ in.
Purchase, Evelyn Kranes Kossak Gift, 2006   2006.240

The Fortune Teller
Georges de La Tour, French, 1593–1652
Oil on canvas, 40⅛ x 48⅝ in., probably 1630s
Rogers Fund, 1960   60.30

Lair of the Sea Serpent
Elihu Vedder, American, 1836–1923
Oil on canvas, 12 x 30 in., ca. 1899
Gift of Mrs. Harold G. Henderson, 1976
1976.106.1

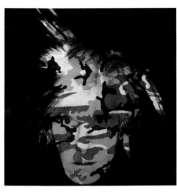

Self-Portrait
Andy Warhol, American, 1928–1987
Acrylic and silkscreen on canvas, 80 x 80 in., 1986
Purchase, Mrs. Vera G. List Gift, 1987   1987.88
© 2009 The Andy Warhol Foundation for the
Visual Arts / Artists Rights Society (ARS), New York

The Titan's Goblet
Thomas Cole, American, 1801–1848
Oil on canvas, 19⅜ x 16⅛ in., 1833
Gift of Samuel P. Avery Jr., 1904   04.29.2

Dancers Practicing at the Barre
Edgar Degas, French, 1834–1917
Mixed media on canvas, 29¾ x 32 in., 1877
H. O. Havemeyer Collection, Bequest of
Mrs. H. O. Havemeyer, 1929   29.100.34

The Sixteen Luohans (detail)
Wu Bin, Chinese, active ca. 1583–1626
Handscroll; ink and color on paper,
12⅝ in. x 13 ft. 7⅛ in., 1591
Edward Elliott Family Collection, Gift of
Douglas Dillon, 1986   1986.266.4

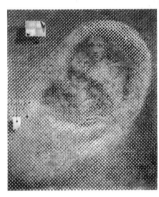

Madonna
Salvador Dali, Spanish, 1904–1989
Oil on canvas, 88⅞ x 75¼ in., 1958
Gift of Drue Heinz, in memory of
Henry J. Heinz II, 1987   1987.465
© 2009 Salvador Dalí, Gala-Salvador
Dali Foundation / Artists Rights Society
(ARS), New York

A Fox Dance from the Drama The
Thousand Cherry Trees
Ippitsusai Bunchō, Japanese, 1723–1792
Polychrome woodblock print; ink and
color on paper, 11⅝ x 5⅝ in.
H. O. Havemeyer Collection, Bequest of
Mrs. H. O. Havemeyer, 1929   JP1777

*The Royal Allied Oak and Self-Created
Mushroom Kings*
Attributed to William Heath, British, 1795–1840,
after J. Field, British, early 19th century;
published by J. Jenkins, London
Hand-colored etching, 14¹⁵⁄₁₆ x 10¹³⁄₁₆ in., 1815
The Glenn Tilley Morse Collection, Bequest of
Glenn Tilley Morse, 1950   50.602.200

*A Goldsmith in His Shop, Possibly
Saint Eligius*
Petrus Christus, Netherlandish, active by
1444, died 1475/76
Oil on oak panel, 39⅜ x 33¾ in., 1449
Robert Lehman Collection, 1975   1975.1.110

Composite Camel with Attendant
Attributed to Uzbekistan (Bukhara), Safavid
Period (1501–1722), 16th century
Gouache on paper, 8⅝ x 6¼ in.
Gift of George D. Pratt, 1925   25.83.6

First published in the United Kingdom in 2009 by
Thames & Hudson Ltd, 181A High Holborn,
London WC1V 7QX

www.thamesandhudson.com

Produced by the Department of Special Publications, The Metropolitan Museum of Art:
Robie Rogge, Publishing Manager; text by Linda C. Falken, Senior Editor; Atif Toor, Designer; Gillian Moran, Production Associate.
Photography by The Metropolitan Museum of Art Photograph Studio, except where noted otherwise.

Visit the Museum's website: www.metmuseum.org

British Library Cataloguing-in-Publication Data
A catalogue record for this book is available from the British Library

ISBN: 978-0-500-51475-7

Printed and bound in China